Theory Paper Grade 2   2013   A
Model Answers

1 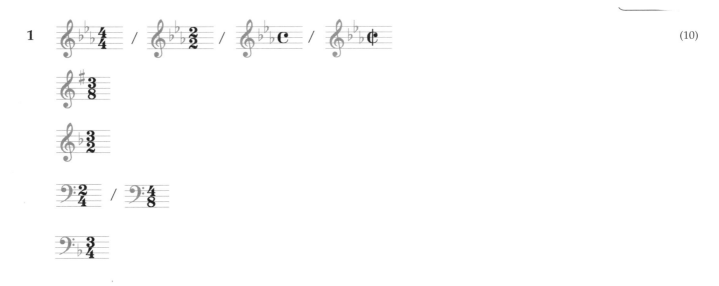 (10)

2 *There are many ways of completing this question. The specimen completion below would receive full marks.* (10)

3 (10)

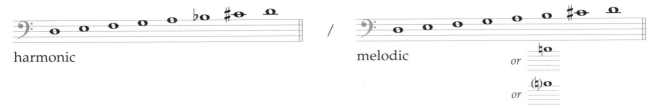

4 (10)

(a)

(b)   D major

5 (10)

6  (10)

7 (10)

8 (a) little / a little / a bit / slightly (10)
fast / quick / cheerful / lively
very quiet / very soft
play the notes detached / jumpy
accent / forced / accented

   (b) (10)
   (i) E
   (ii) C major
   (iii) *There are five possible answers to this question. Any of the answers shown would receive full marks.*

   (iv) 7; 8
   (v) false

   (c) (10)

Theory Paper Grade 2   2013   B
Model Answers

1 (10)

Music Theory
Past Papers
2013
Model Answers

ABRSM Grade 2

Welcome to ABRSM's *Music Theory Past Papers 2013 Model Answers*, Grade 2. These answers are a useful resource for students and teachers preparing for ABRSM theory exams and should be used alongside the relevant published theory past papers.

All the answers in this booklet would receive full marks but not all possible answers have been included for practicable reasons. In these cases other reasonable alternatives may also be awarded full marks. For composition-style questions (where candidates must complete a rhythm, compose a melody based on a given opening or set text to music) only one example of the many possible answers is given.

For more information on how theory papers are marked and some general advice on taking theory exams, please refer to the Music Theory Grade 2 web page: www.abrsm.org/theory2.

Using these answers

- Answers are given in the same order and, where possible, in the same layout as in the exam papers, making it easy to match answer to question.

- Where it is necessary to show the answer on a stave, the original stave is printed in grey with the answer shown in black, for example:

- Alternative answers are separated by an oblique stroke (/) or by *or*, for example:

  getting slower / gradually getting slower

- Answers that require the candidate to write out a scale or chord have been shown at one octave only. Reasonable alternatives at different octaves can also receive full marks.

© 2014 by The Associated Board of the Royal Schools of Music
Published by ABRSM (Publishing) Ltd, a wholly owned subsidiary of ABRSM
Cover by Kate Benjamin & Andy Potts
Printed in England by Page Bros (Norwich) Ltd

2 *There are many ways of completing this question. The specimen completion below would receive full marks.* (10)

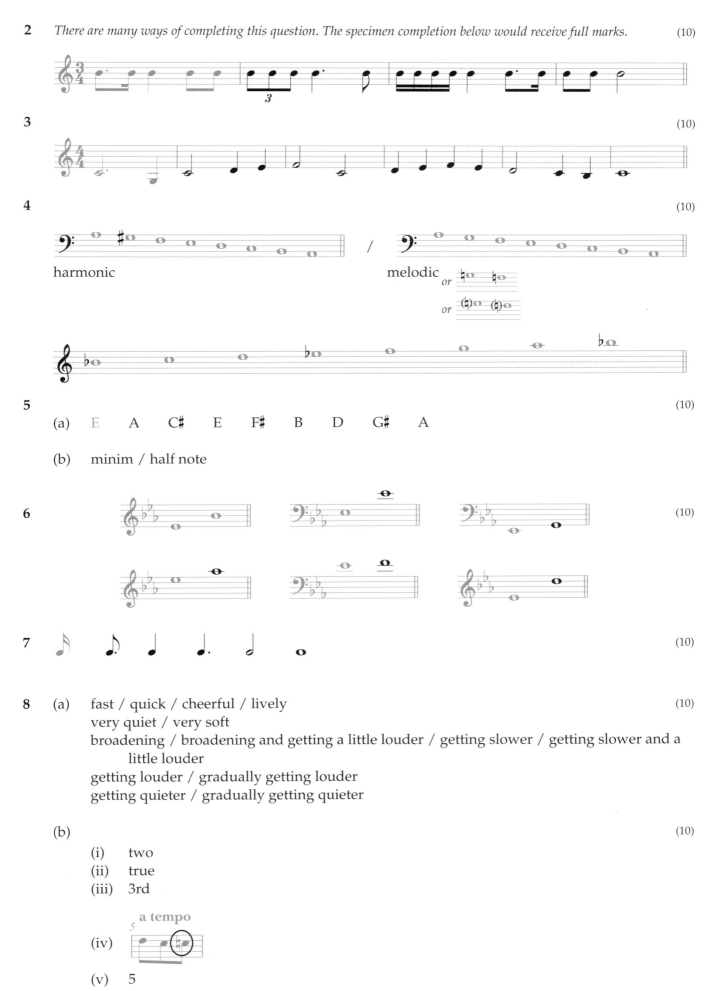

3 (10)

4 (10)

harmonic

melodic *or*

or

5 (10)

(a) E   A   C#   E   F#   B   D   G#   A

(b) minim / half note

6 (10)

7 (10)

8 (a) fast / quick / cheerful / lively (10)
very quiet / very soft
broadening / broadening and getting a little louder / getting slower / getting slower and a little louder
getting louder / gradually getting louder
getting quieter / gradually getting quieter

(b) (10)

    (i)   two
    (ii)   true
    (iii) 3rd

    (iv)

    (v)   5

(c)

Theory Paper Grade 2   2013   C
Model Answers

1 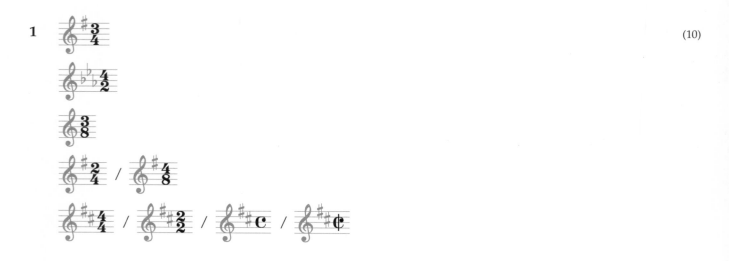 (10)

2 *There are many ways of completing this question. The specimen completion below would receive full marks.* (10)

3 B♭ A E (10)
E♭ D A

4 3rd 6th 5th (10)
7th 4th 8th / 8ve

5 (10)

(a) 2nd 3rd 5th 7th 8th / 6th 4th 2nd 1st /
8ve / 1st 8th / 8ve

(b) six

6 (10)

7 (10)

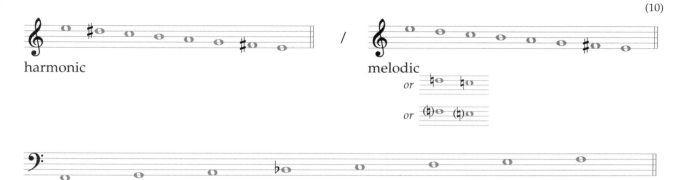

harmonic

melodic

or

or

8 (a) at a walking pace / medium speed (10)
much / very
play the notes smoothly / slur
quiet / soft
getting louder / gradually getting louder

(b) (10)

(i) **Andante e molto legato**

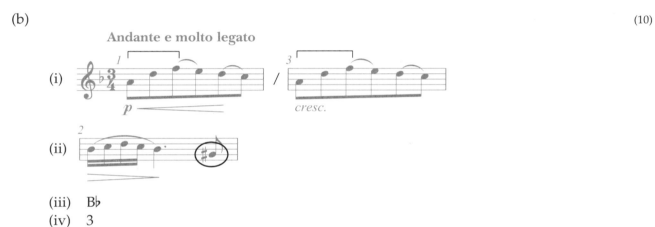

(ii)

(iii) B♭

(iv) 3

(v) four

(c) (10)

Theory Paper Grade 2   2013   S
Model Answers

1 (10)

2 *There are many ways of completing this question. The specimen completion below would receive full marks.* (10)

3 (10)

(a) 5th   6th   1st /   8th /   2nd   5th   7th   4th   3rd
           8th / 8ve   8ve / 1st

(b) quaver / eighth note

4 (10)

5 (10)

6 5th   7th   4th (10)
      3rd   2nd   6th

7 (10)

8   (a)   fairly quick / quite quick / quick, but not as quick as Allegro   (10)
sweet / soft / gentle
getting quieter / gradually getting quieter
quiet / soft
go back to the beginning and repeat the section / repeat the passage from the beginning

(b)   (10)

(i)   7
(ii)   true
(iii) C
(iv)   *legato* (smoothly)

(v)   six

(c)      (10)

Music Theory Past Papers 2013 Model Answers

Model answers for four past papers from ABRSM's 2013 Theory exams for Grade 2

Key features:

- a list of correct answers where appropriate
- a selection of likely options where the answer can be expressed in a variety of ways
- a single exemplar where a composition-style answer is required

Support material for ABRSM Theory exams

ABRSM
24 Portland Place
London W1B 1LU
United Kingdom

www.abrsm.org

ABRSM is the exam board of the Royal Schools of Music. We are committed to actively supporting high-quality music-making, learning and development throughout the world, and to producing the best possible resources for music teachers and students.

ISBN 978-1-84849-615-6

9 781848 496156